The Glory of Bethlehem

Brian R. Keller

NORTHWESTERN PUBLISHING HOUSE
Milwaukee, Wisconsin

Scripture is taken from the HOLY BIBLE, NEW INTERNATIONAL VERSION®. Copyright © 1973, 1978, 1984 by International Bible Society. Used by permission of Zondervan Publishing House. All rights reserved.

The "NIV" and "New International Version" trademarks are registered in the United States Patent and Trademark Office by International Bible Society. Use of either trademark requires the permission of International Bible Society.

All rights reserved. No part of this publication may be reproduced, stored in a retrieval system, or transmitted in any form or by any means—electronic, mechanical, photocopying, recording, or otherwise— except for brief quotations in reviews, without prior permission from the publisher.

Northwestern Publishing House
1250 N. 113th St., Milwaukee, WI 53226-3284
www.nph.net
© 2005 by Northwestern Publishing House
Published 2005
Printed in the United States of America
ISBN-13: 978-0-8100-1665-6
ISBN-10: 0-8100-1665-6

A Gift To

_____

From

_____

The Glory of Bethlehem

Luke 2

The Setting

In those days Caesar Augustus issued a decree that a census should be taken of the entire Roman world. (This was the first census that took place while Quirinius was governor of Syria.) And everyone went to his own town to register.

So Joseph also went up from the town of Nazareth in Galilee to Judea, to Bethlehem the town of David, because he belonged to the house and line of David. **(Luke 2:1-4)**

What do you think of when you hear the word *Christmas*? Many Americans probably think of the secular customs that are now attached to the Christmas holiday season. A Christmas tree lit with lights and adorned with beautiful decorations, vivid colors of red and green blending with falling snow, and a sumptuous feast—these things virtually cry out, "It's Christmas!" Certain songs and tunes heard in malls and stores are readily recognized as Christmas music. But does that music really flow from the true meaning of Christmas? Or is it just produced in the interests of commercialism?

As a pastor, I find that Christmas services are attended by more people than any other service. We decorate our churches with trees and lights. There is almost a hustle-and-bustle feeling in our buildings as children, choirs, and musicians prepare for the festival worship services. Is that what you think of when you hear the word *Christmas*?

The setting of our Savior's birth was rather different than that to which most Americans are accustomed today. Let's try to picture what it was like for Joseph and Mary long ago. We cannot be certain about some of the details. Was Jesus born on December 25? Was it wintry weather? Did Joseph walk as Mary rode on a donkey? We do not know.

Joseph and Mary must have traveled for several days from Nazareth to Bethlehem. In obedience to the government, Joseph went to the town of his family to be counted in a census, probably for taxation purposes. Both Joseph and Mary were descendants of King David, and Bethlehem was David's hometown.

God had made many promises to send a Savior from sin. Immediately after Adam and Eve had committed the first sin, God had promised that a Redeemer would be born of a woman and would crush the power of Satan, opening to all the door to heaven (Genesis 3:15).

Through the prophet Micah, God had foretold our Savior's birthplace: "But you, Bethlehem Ephrathah, though you are small among the clans of Judah, out of you will come for me one who will be ruler over Israel, whose origins are from of old, from days of eternity" (5:2—using the translation suggested by the NIV footnote). This states that the Savior would come from eternity, but he would be born in Bethlehem. (Actually, there were two towns with this name, one in the north and one in the south. The Messiah would be born in the Bethlehem in the south—that's what "Ephrathah" tells us.)

Each year we sing the well-known Christmas hymn "O Little Town of Bethlehem" (*Christian Worship* [CW] 65) and recall how our Savior was born in that lowly place and in the humble circumstances that place afforded him. When Joseph and Mary entered Bethlehem, the world hardly noticed at all. In fact, most didn't notice. Who would have suspected that the eternal Son of God would be born in that place and in that way?

God doesn't always do things as we might expect. This was one of those times. The setting of our Savior's birth reminds us that God does not overlook humble people in lowly places.

Whether we spend Christmas with family and

friends in a familiar place or apart from them in an unfamiliar place, the Lord is still with us as we remember in faith our Savior's birth. Whether we worship with a large congregation in wintry weather or with a small congregation in a warmer climate, Christmas comes just the same. Many Christmas memories cannot be duplicated, but the real meaning of Christmas always remains. Wherever we are and in whatever circumstances, the important part of Christmas is worshiping God's Son, our Savior, Jesus Christ.

The Virgin

He went there to register with Mary, who was pledged to be married to him and was expecting a child. **(Luke 2:5)**

It was probably good for Mary to escape the situation in Nazareth. Just imagine what people would have said about a virgin who had become pregnant. Her reputation must have suffered.

While she was still in Nazareth, Mary was "pledged to be married" to Joseph (*betrothal*). At that time, a betrothal included vows as binding as today's marriage ceremony. No extra vows were needed for them to be married. At the appointed time, the husband could take his wife home. Joseph and Mary were married, and Mary was "his wife" already in Nazareth, months before they arrived in Bethlehem. But Joseph "had no union with her until she gave birth to a son" (Matthew 1:25). In this unique situation, although Mary was Joseph's wife, she was still a virgin when she arrived in Bethlehem and gave birth to our Savior.

The fact that Jesus was conceived and born of a virgin fulfilled another prophecy of the Old Testament Scriptures. Isaiah prophesied: "Therefore the Lord himself will give you a sign: The virgin will be with child and will give birth to a son, and will call him Immanuel" (7:14). Mary was "the virgin" who had been "with child" and had given "birth to a son." There has been no other time when a virgin has conceived and has given birth. Mary is the only fulfillment of Isaiah's words. Through the prophet Isaiah, God directly foretold of the virgin birth of Christ.

And yes, virgin means that she had never had sexual relations with a man. Each time this Hebrew term occurs in Scripture it refers to a woman who is still a virgin. Some Bible versions translate the word in Isaiah 7:14 as "young woman" instead of "virgin." Perhaps this is due to a bias of the translators. However, even if the Hebrew term could mean "young woman" and not necessarily "virgin," the Holy Spirit left no doubt how we are to understand it in Isaiah's passage. Matthew 1:22,23 plainly declares, "All this [everything revolving around Mary's pregnancy and the angel's message to Joseph] took place to fulfill what the Lord had said through the prophet: 'The virgin will be with child and will give birth to a son, and they will call him Immanuel'—which means, 'God with us.'"

We need to be careful that we do not add to or subtract from God's Word. Dangerous false teachers deny this prophecy and its fulfillment. Satan would like to have us deny this part of God's Word, because he wants to attack our Savior and his rightful glory. He would like to have us think that Christ was not born of a virgin, that he was just a sinner like the rest of us. Our sinful flesh doesn't help our belief either, because a virgin birth does not agree with our human reason. No one else has been born of a virgin! This doesn't happen every day!

Other dangerous false teachers have gone too far the other way, saying more about Mary than is right. They have claimed that she was born holy, like Jesus. But Mary was not perfect or sinless. She too needed a Savior from sin. We should not worship Mary or pray to her. The First Commandment forbids that!

But the fact that many people pray to Mary is not her fault. We have no record of her even hinting that people should pray to her. Yes, she was the mother of our Lord. Yes, God was gracious to her. But she was not a coRedeemer with Jesus.

Instead of praising Mary, we should praise God for giving and keeping his marvelous and miraculous promise to send our Savior via "the virgin." In this way, our Savior entered our world without inherited sin. In this way, Jesus became the God-man. In this way, God came into the world to keep the law perfectly as one of us. In this way, God came to this earth to die for our sins.

God always keeps his promises. He kept his amazing promise about the virgin birth. He'll keep this one too: "Whoever believes in [Jesus] shall not perish but have eternal life" (John 3:16).

The Time

***While they were there, the time came for the baby to be born.* (Luke 2:6)**

Children really look forward to Christmas, don't they? Can you remember the feeling of anticipation you had when you were younger? You could hardly wait!

In some homes, children are not permitted to open their presents until Christmas Eve or Christmas Day. It seems like torture, but when this custom is properly understood, it can teach a valuable lesson about the first Christmas. God's promise of his gift to us was given at first in the Garden of Eden (Genesis 3:15) and continued to be repeated by prophets throughout the Old Testament. God's people had to wait a long time, a very long time, for the Savior to arrive!

Mary waited too. We might wish for more details about Mary's pregnancy than Scripture provides, but God has decided that it is not important for us to know whether or not Mary got morning sickness or how long she was in labor. From the way Luke records the birth, we can safely assume hers was a full-term pregnancy. Women who have been pregnant know what it's like when the days of pregnancy are over. The days were completed for Mary to be delivered from the difficulties of pregnancy. After much waiting, it was time for the Savior to be born.

During those days of pregnancy, God does amazing miracles in the womb. Yet isn't it even more amazing that the Son of God waited patiently and humbly in the womb for some nine months? He certainly could have thought of an easier way to enter our world.

We don't know for sure how long Joseph and Mary had been in Bethlehem before the Christ was born. It must not have been too long—perhaps a few hours or days. All we know for sure is that "the time came" while they were in Bethlehem. Joseph must have wanted to get his pregnant wife into a comfortable bed in an inn. But they were still living in a stable when Jesus was born.

There was much more behind the proper timing of Jesus' birth than one might realize with a superficial reading of Scripture. The Roman decree of a census needed to be timed perfectly, perhaps taking into account some organizational delays, so that Joseph and Mary would have to leave Nazareth for Bethlehem just in time for the promise of Micah 5:2 to be fulfilled: "But you, Bethlehem Ephrathah, though you are small among the clans of Judah, out of you will come for me one who will be ruler over Israel."

This was the right time for our Redeemer to be born, for his gospel to be spread easily and quickly throughout the world. There were good Roman roads on which the missionaries could travel. The Greek language served as a common language for the New Testament writers. There were probably many reasons why God determined that this was the time for the Savior to be born. It was the right time because the Lord decided that the time was right and that it was in keeping with his whole plan for the world and his kingdom.

The inspired apostle Paul put it this way: "When the time had fully come, God sent his Son, born of a woman, born under law, to redeem those under law, that we might receive the full rights of sons" (Galatians 4:4,5). When the time was just right, God the Father sent his only-begotten Son to be born of the virgin Mary. This happened so that our Redeemer could be born under the law, obey it perfectly for us, and then offer himself as the atoning sacrifice for the sins of the whole world. Consequently, we believers are God's children and heirs of the kingdom of heaven. Thanks and praise to the triune God, who carried out his plan at just the right time.

The Birth

And she gave birth to her firstborn, a son. (Luke 2:7)

What was the best Christmas gift you ever received? Maybe it was a shiny new bicycle or a video game. Most American adults would probably remember an expensive gift like jewelry or a major tool.

But how would you answer that question from the bottom of your heart? Would you agree that the greatest Christmas gift we ever received was our Savior, Jesus Christ?

People who do not believe will think that to

be a strange reply. Think about it. The baby Jesus looked no different than any other baby. If anything, his birth was less impressive than most others. Most births at that time were in homes. Kings would have been born in palaces. And babies today are born in well-appointed hospitals. But Jesus was born in a barn. Actually, it was a stable, where animals were sheltered. Many scholars believe that the stable was actually a cave.

The best Christmas gift one could ever receive? Really? Even the wording of Luke chapter 2 sounds more simple than impressive.

Isn't it a wonder that God can take the great miracle of our Savior's birth and make it sound so simple? The words are not filled with flowery praise or technical jargon. It is not how a human author would record such an event. Miracles are meant to be expanded on and played up, aren't they? Luke's account is different. It is humble, just like Jesus' birth. It is straightforward in announcing the birth of God's Son—our greatest Christmas gift ever.

We need this gift more than any other. Without a Savior, we would all perish eternally because of our sins. Without this Savior, God would justly reject us forever. Without the birth of Jesus, we would have no hope of enjoying heaven for all eternity. That's why this is the greatest Christmas gift ever.

What's more, God didn't send this gift only to a select group of people. God gave this gift to the entire world. "For God so loved the *world* that he gave his one and only Son, that whoever believes in him shall not perish but have eternal life" (John 3:16). God demonstrated his love for the whole world—for all people of all times—when he sent his "one and only Son" to be born as our Savior.

God "wants all men to be saved and to come to a knowledge of the truth" (1 Timothy 2:4). He wants everyone to know that Jesus was born for all people and redeemed all people. God wants all people to believe in Jesus Christ as their Savior from sin, for he said, "Whoever believes in him shall not perish but have eternal life."

That is what makes Jesus the best Christmas gift we have ever received or will ever receive. We deserve to perish because of our sins against God. We do not obey his commands perfectly, and that is what God expects of us. Unless we are absolutely holy, without any stains of sin, we cannot go to heaven. But God knows that we can't be perfect! No one is perfect! No one, that is, except Jesus, who was born to redeem us. He lived a perfect life for us and died on the cross to pay for all sin. He rose from death because he earned forgiveness for all sinners, so that by faith in him we would have eternal life.

We were on our way to eternal punishment, but through Jesus we are on our way to eternal life in heaven!

I'd say that makes him the greatest Christmas gift we can ever receive, wouldn't you?

The Humility of God's Son

***She wrapped him in cloths and placed him in a manger, because there was no room for them in the inn.* (Luke 2:7)**

If you were told that God's Son had been born and that he needed a place to rest, where would you put him? Most likely, you would take him to the very best hospital or a fine five-star hotel. You surely would not put him in a place where animals eat. But that's where his parents put Jesus right after he was born.

It seems that his mother delivered Jesus without much help. We are not told that a midwife was there. Mary was the one who wrapped Jesus in swaddling clothes, or strips of cloth. In Luther's day, people actually claimed to still have the strips of cloth, which they claimed were made from Joseph's trousers.

Some writers describe the scene as though they were there, but we really don't know any more than what the inspired Scriptures tell us. Did the manger scene look like the manger scenes we display at Christmas on our lawns and in our homes? We cannot be sure.

A manger was a feeding trough for animals. That was our Savior's first crib. We are told that there was "no room for them in the inn." We don't know what the inn was like. Perhaps, as one author wrote, it was "a public stopping place covered with a roof and having in its one room a number of stalls, ranged one beside the other along the walls, where the travelers could lodge and rest, while in the middle of the room space was provided for the beasts of burden, and mangers were installed for them."[1]

Regardless of how we picture it, it is not important that we know all the details. If it were, God would have provided that information in the Bible. What is important is that Jesus was born to be our Savior and that he was born in humble circumstances.

No matter how we picture the manger scene, it was not a place we would select as appropriate for the Son of God, at least according to our way of thinking. Remember, "in Christ all the fullness of the Deity

---

[1] Arndt, William F. *Luke*. St. Louis: Concordia, 1956, p. 74.

lives in bodily form" (Colossians 2:9). This baby in the manger was true God and true man in one person!

When the Son of God was conceived by the Holy Spirit and born of the virgin Mary, he became true man—he became the God-man. However, even when he became true man, God's Son never stopped being true God. Even after Jesus rose from the dead and ascended into heaven as true God, he was still a true man. "For there is one God and one mediator between God and men, the man Christ Jesus" (1 Timothy 2:5).

Christians all know that Jesus humbled himself, but many have the misconception that he humbled himself by becoming incarnate, that is, by becoming a human being with flesh and blood like us. But becoming flesh and blood was not part of Jesus' humiliation. If that were so, he would have stopped being a man after his time of humiliation and suffering were over.

It is the lowly manner of Jesus' birth that is part of his humiliation. Even though this baby was "in very nature God," he willingly chose to be born in such a lowly place and to use a feeding trough for his first bed (Philippians 2:6). The Son of God did not enter our world to show off, to flaunt the glory that was always his. On the contrary, he entered this world as a humble, suffering servant to redeem us. In the end, he humbled himself to the point of dying on a cross. There he became the atoning sacrifice for our sins.

Gentle Mary laid her child
Lowly in a manger;
He is still the undefiled,
But no more a stranger.
Son of God, of humble birth,
Beautiful the story;
Praise his name in all the earth,
Hail the King of glory! (CW 56:3)

The Shepherds

And there were shepherds living out in the fields nearby, keeping watch over their flocks at night. (Luke 2:8)

I recall watching a show on television that used the phrase, "Meanwhile, back at the ranch." Something would be happening in two different places, and the scene would switch from one place to the other. That is essentially what Luke does here. Jesus had just been born in Bethlehem. Mary had just "wrapped him in cloths and placed him in a manger" (verse 7). And then, it's almost as if the Bible text says, "Meanwhile, out in the fields . . . there were shepherds keeping watch over their flocks."

If this would happen today, we would have television crews setting up satellite links and broadcasting the news all over the world. We would expect instant visits from important dignitaries. We would expect emperors, kings, and high priests to be informed of the birth before anyone else.

But the first people to learn of the Savior's birth were lowly shepherds "living out in the fields nearby."

The Jews did not think too highly of shepherds. Students of history say that shepherds had a low reputation at the time. One rabbi expressed surprise that God could be compared to a shepherd, as he is in Psalm 23. Shepherds were often treated as social outcasts. Imagine that! The gospel first went to social outcasts.

But this was God's way. The inspired apostle Paul said: "Brothers, think of what you were when you were called. Not many of you were wise by human standards; not many were influential; not many were of noble birth. But God chose the foolish things of the world to shame the wise; God chose the weak things of the world to shame the strong. He chose the lowly things of this world and the despised things—and the things that are not—to nullify the things that are, so that no one may boast before him" (1 Corinthians 1:26-29).

God was gracious to those shepherds. He has been gracious to us too. How wonderful it is to know what Christmas is really all about! How blessed we are to know that our Savior was born in the little town of Bethlehem! It is only because of God's amazing grace that we have heard this good news of great joy.

Do we really appreciate God's grace? He planned our salvation and promised a Savior. He sent a Savior who redeemed us from sin. He gave us this good news and the faith to believe it. He has promised an eternal home in heaven to all who believe in Jesus.

What grace God has shown to sinners like you and me! Scripture declares, "For it is by grace you have been saved, through faith—and this not from yourselves, it is the gift of God—not by works, so that no one can boast" (Ephesians 2:8,9). The hymn writer Christian Scheidt summarized these thoughts in this way:

By grace God's Son, our only Savior,
Came down to earth to bear our sin.
Was it because of your own merit
That Jesus died your soul to win?
No, it was grace, and grace alone,
That brought him from his heav'nly throne.

(CW 384:2)

The Angel and the Glory of the Lord

An angel of the Lord appeared to them, and the glory of the Lord shone around them, and they were terrified. (Luke 2:9)

Have you ever been so startled that you felt instant terror? Perhaps you were startled by sounds in the night. Perhaps someone or something came upon you suddenly. Perhaps a person unexpectedly came around a corner or an animal suddenly came out of the woods as you were hiking.

Try to imagine what it must have been like for those "shepherds living out in the fields nearby, keeping watch over their flocks at night" (Luke 2:8). There they were, doing their work out in the darkness, when suddenly they were confronted by an angel and the brilliant glory of the Lord!

Not many people have seen angels, but those who have are often described in Scripture as being terrified. When an angel of the Lord appeared to Zechariah, the father of John the Baptist, we are told that "he was startled and was gripped with fear" (Luke 1:12). On Easter Sunday, when Jesus rose from death, "There was a violent earthquake, for an angel of the Lord came down from heaven and, going to the tomb, rolled back the stone and sat on it. His appearance was like lightning, and his clothes were white as snow. The guards were so afraid of him that they shook and became like dead men" (Matthew 28:2-4). If brave Roman guards could be afraid of angels, so could the shepherds. Luke says, "They were terrified."

But it was not just the angel that made them afraid. They were terrified of being in the presence of God. "The glory of the Lord shone around them." In the Old Testament, the phrase "the glory of the LORD" indicates the special visible presence of God. For examples, see Exodus 16:10; 24:15-17; 40:34. Scripture reveals that "the glory of the LORD looked like a consuming fire" (Exodus 24:17). This visible presence of the Lord "shone around" the shepherds, and they were "terrified."

Of what were they afraid? Was it just that they had been startled? Was it fear of the unknown? Or was it the kind of fear that sinners always feel when confronted by the sheer blinding holiness of God? It was perhaps a combination of all these things. But the last reason, no doubt, was the most important.

The angel's sudden appearance was not meant to startle the shepherds, however. As we hear in the next verse, the angel had good news for them. He came to tell the shepherds about the birth of the Savior.

Isn't it great to know that we believers don't have to be afraid of God's judgment? We know that if we would try to stand before God simply on the basis of our own thoughts, words, and the supposed goodness of our own lives, we would have good reason to be terrified. All people are sinners. All sinners deserve eternal condemnation from God. But God sent his Son to save us.

Jesus reconciled sinners with God by living a sinless life and offering that life on the cross as the complete sacrifice for the world's sins. He rose from the dead because he accomplished his mission of redeeming us. Whoever believes in Jesus, our Savior from sin, has no need to be afraid of God. Instead, by faith in Christ we are God's own children! We believers are heirs of the eternal kingdom of heaven. As the angel said, "Do not be afraid."

The Recipients of the Good News

But the angel said to them, "Do not be afraid. I bring you good news of great joy that will be for all the people." (Luke 2:10)

When we hear the law, we should always be afraid. Hearing what God has commanded and realizing that we have not kept his commands leads to fear. After all, God threatens to punish all those who disobey his commands. The law tells us that we all deserve to suffer forever in hell. That is a terrifying message. But the gospel announces God's rescue plan. Because Jesus redeemed all people, whoever believes in him will not perish in hell but will enjoy the perfect world of heaven forever. This good news of forgiveness, life, and salvation makes us glad. The gospel turns fear into "great joy."

For whom is this message? The angel proclaimed the gospel to lowly shepherds first, but he said that this "good news" of salvation through the newborn Christ is intended "for all the people." It was not just for the shepherds. It was not just for the Jews. It is for all people.

God revealed this truth in the Old Testament: the Savior that God promised in the Garden of Eden would come to save all people (Genesis 3:15). The Messiah would be "a light for the Gentiles," and for the Jews as well (Isaiah 42:6). It would be "too small a thing" for the Savior to redeem Israel; he would bring salvation to all, even "the Gentiles" (Isaiah 49:6).

No matter what our family roots may be, the Savior also came for us. We can be sure of this, because he came to redeem all people. That truth makes me even more certain than if God would have written my own name in the Bible. If God had written my name in the Bible, I might wonder if he meant me or someone else who has the same name as mine. But I know that God includes me, because Jesus came to redeem "all the people," and I am included in that group. So are you!

I'm glad the gospel is for all people. I'm glad that "God so loved the world" that he sent his Son to save the world (John 3:16). I'm glad that Jesus came to be "the atoning sacrifice for our sins, and not only for ours but also for the sins of the whole world" (1 John 2:2). The fact that the gospel is for all people gives me comfort and assurance. It also reminds me that the gospel isn't only for me—we still have mission work to do.

Do you ever pause to think about the people who need to hear the gospel? It might be your father-in-law. It might be a neighbor across the street. It might be a coworker. It might be a stranger in your town. It might be someone in a foreign country. There are still people all over the world who have not learned the good news that Jesus paid for their sins on the cross.

How can people believe in Jesus if they've never heard about him? And how can they hear about him unless someone tells them? Maybe you, your pastor, or a missionary will tell them. "As it is written, 'How beautiful are the feet of those who bring good news!'" (Romans 10:15). Thank God that the good news is for all!

The Savior, Christ the Lord

"Today in the town of David a Savior has been born to you; he is Christ the Lord." (Luke 2:11)

This is the heart of this precious passage from God's Word. The angel announced the good news to the shepherds. There was no reason for them to be afraid. The angel was bringing the kind of news that brings joy.

The angel brought the shepherds current, late-breaking news. Something had just happened nearby in Bethlehem. "Today in the town of David a Savior has been born to you." The Savior had been born! He was born "to you" and for you. Rejoice and be glad, your Savior was born!

The long-promised Savior from sin had finally arrived. He would be called Jesus, because he would "save his people from their sins" (Matthew 1:21). That's the kind of Savior that Jesus is. That's the kind of Savior we really need. He was born to rescue people from the eternal consequences of sin. This was the work his Father gave him to do.

Now consider what kind of person Jesus was

and is. According to his human nature, Jesus had a birthday. He was "conceived by the Holy Spirit and born of the virgin Mary." According to his divine nature, however, Jesus had no beginning. The eternal Son of God always existed. This fact impresses on us just who Jesus is: true God and true man in one person, "he is Christ the Lord."

Remarkably, all of this came to light seven centuries earlier through the inspired writings of the prophet Micah: "But you, Bethlehem Ephrathah, though you are small among the clans of Judah, out of you will come for me one who will be ruler over Israel, whose origins are from of old, from days of eternity" (5:2[2]). In this verse the Lord revealed that the birthplace of our Savior would be Bethlehem Ephrathah (David's hometown). This verse also revealed that the Savior is eternal. God's Son would be born in Bethlehem, but he really had no beginning at all. He always existed—"from days of eternity."

Jesus, the God-man, lived perfectly, died on a cross, and rose from the dead as our Savior from sin. He did this for you, for me, and for all people. Let us worship him! "He is Christ," the anointed Savior

---

[2]Translation from NIV footnote. Beck's AAT says, "Who comes from eternity."

from sin. (*Christ* means "anointed one" in Greek. It is the same word as *Messiah* in Hebrew). He is the Lord, the God who revealed himself by that name in the Old Testament (Exodus 34:6,7).

Isaiah announced the good news of Christmas seven hundred years before it happened: "For to us a child is born, to us a son is given, and the government will be on his shoulders. And he will be called Wonderful Counselor, Mighty God, Everlasting Father, Prince of Peace" (9:6). That's Jesus! He is the "Mighty God" who comforts us with the gospel of peace through his forgiveness.

God from true God, and Light from Light eternal,
Born of a virgin, to earth he comes,
Only begotten Son of God the Father.
Oh, come, let us adore him,
Oh, come, let us adore him,
Oh, come, let us adore him,
Christ the Lord. (CW 55:2)

The Sign

"This will be a sign to you: You will find a baby wrapped in cloths and lying in a manger." (Luke 2:12)

Our highways are dotted with signs. Signs indicate what is coming up. Signs mark important places—where famous battles were fought or where famous people lived. I recall that my grandparents always stopped to read landmark signs along the road. But most of us drive past many signs without giving them a second thought.

The sign marking our Savior's birth can no longer be seen. Oh sure, if you travel to Bethlehem today, there are signs that point to where people think Jesus was born. But we can't be sure. The angel who appeared to the shepherds gave the real sign pointing to where our Savior was born. The angel told the shepherds, "You will find a baby wrapped in cloths and lying in a manger." The shepherds were to look for a baby wrapped in strips of cloth and lying in a trough for feeding cattle. The shepherds would have little trouble finding such a baby in the little town of Bethlehem.

And yet, it must have seemed strange to them. The Savior's birth was so important that God used angels to announce it, but the shepherds were not told to look in a palace but in a stable. They were not to look for a bed of gold. They were to look for a baby "lying in a manger."

Jesus had come to identify with lowly sinners. He did not come to show off or live a life of ease. "The Son of Man did not come to be served, but to serve, and to give his life as a ransom for many" (Matthew 20:28). Jesus served us by taking on himself the guilt of our sins and then suffering and dying for them. He humbled himself even to the point of death on a cross!

In keeping with our Savior's humility, a gaudy sign with flashing arrows in bright lights did not point out the place of our Savior's birth. The sign was a manger—the baby Jesus was wrapped in swaddling clothes and lying in a feeding trough. "Away in a manger, no crib for a bed, the little Lord Jesus laid down his sweet head" (CW 68:1).

Do you pause each Christmas to meditate on this sign of our Savior's birth? Could the Savior of the world be born like this? One hymn writer put it this way:

Gentle Mary laid her child
Lowly in a manger;
There he lay, the undefiled,
To the world a stranger.
Such a babe in such a place—
Can he be the Savior? (CW 56:1)

Yes, Jesus is the Savior. His sign is humility. Though Jesus was born in a humble way, one day he will return in great glory. Right now Jesus is ruling over the whole universe. He is the almighty Son of

God, sitting at God's right hand. He was humble enough to redeem us. Let us worship him. He deserves our glory and praise.

The Song of Praise

Suddenly a great company of the heavenly host appeared with the angel, praising God and saying, "Glory to God in the highest, and on earth peace to men on whom his favor rests." (Luke 2:13,14)

The shepherds had heard the good news and had learned how they could find the Savior. Now they would have the rare opportunity to hear a heavenly choir of angels praising God. There have not been many people blessed with the chance to hear such heavenly praise. Isaiah heard angels praise God with the words, "Holy, holy, holy is the LORD Almighty; the whole earth is full of his glory" (Isaiah 6:3). Can you even imagine what it must be like to hear the holy angels worship God? No choir on earth could ever compare to the angels' perfect melodies.

The shepherds heard a choir made up of many angels. These angels appeared suddenly and joined the angel who had just been talking to the shepherds. This "great company of the heavenly host" joined the first angel in "praising God." The church continues to sing their glorious song of praise. It is the part of our liturgy known as *Gloria in Excelsis Deo* (which is Latin for "Glory to God in the highest").

Notice how the song alternates between God and man, heaven and earth. Glory to God. Peace to men. There is no doubt in the angels' song of praise. They do not merely *hope* that we will give God the glory. God definitely is glorified in sending his Son. They declare "peace to men," because God was providing peace through the Savior, Jesus Christ.[3] Salvation is entirely by God's grace (his love given to sinners who don't deserve it). There is nothing in any of us that made God provide peace through Jesus. Our sins make us God's enemies. We deserve God's punishment for our sins. We do not deserve peace with God or a place in heaven. Yet, by God's grace, that is exactly what Jesus won for us and the whole world. God was in Christ "reconciling the world to himself," bringing about peace (2 Corinthians 5:19). As individuals, we receive and possess this peace with God through faith in Jesus. We read in Romans 5:1, "Therefore, since we have been justified through faith, we have peace with God through our Lord Jesus

---

[3]To learn more from Scripture about this peace, see the following Bible passages: Luke 2:29; Luke 24:36; John 14:27; John 16:33; Acts 10:36; Romans 5:1; Ephesians 2:13-18; Colossians 1:20-22.

Christ," that is, through our Redeemer's holy life and sacrificial death. This gives us good reason to praise God as the angels did.

Today so much of what is called worship seems to be little more than entertainment. But the angels were not out to entertain people. They were "praising God." And, remember, they were not even the ones saved by Christ; we are! We have even more reasons to praise God than the angels did. We should be even more eager to praise him.

One year our church choir prepared to sing parts of Handel's "Messiah" for our Christmas Day worship service. The day was so snowy that many people couldn't come to church. Yet it was still worth it. Not a second of practice had been in vain. It was too bad that more people were not present to hear the music. Yet we were not putting on a performance to please our people. We were praising God.

The greatest choir in history did not have much of an audience either—just some lowly shepherds and flocks of sheep. But it praised God with all its might! God heard the angels' praise and accepted it. For that reason they had the greatest audience in history!

May we too always praise our Savior-God. He has covered us with favor, treated us with mercy, and saved us by pure grace.

The Manger Scene

When the angels had left them and gone into heaven, the shepherds said to one another, "Let's go to Bethlehem and see this thing that has happened, which the Lord has told us about."

So they hurried off and found Mary and Joseph, and the baby, who was lying in the manger.
(Luke 2:15,16)

The angels didn't remain there long, but neither did the shepherds. The angels returned to heaven. The shepherds went to Bethlehem to see the newborn Savior. They went to see what "the Lord" had told them about. They knew that the angel had been God's messenger.

The shepherds didn't drag their feet and make excuses. They could have said that they needed to watch the sheep. They could have put it off for the next day. But they did not linger in the fields. "They hurried off." They were eager to see the Savior. They left their flocks behind and rushed to find the child matching the description given to them by the angels.

We don't know how much the shepherds had to search to find baby Jesus. Did they need to ask a few of the locals if they had seen anything unusual? Or was it obvious to the shepherds where they should look first? We don't know. But we do know this. They followed the angel's directions and found the Christ Child. They "found Mary and Joseph, and the baby, who was lying in the manger."

Just try to imagine what they saw. Can you picture it? To this day many manger scenes try to depict it. The shepherds saw the Son of God as a little baby.

We don't read about the Magi (wise men) being there. That's because they were not at the manger. They arrived considerably later, when our Lord was living in a "house" (Matthew 2:11). It would be more accurate if manger scenes did not place the Magi at the manger.

The first Christmas scene consisted of Mary, Joseph, the shepherds, and Jesus. There were probably animals around. We don't know if any other people were there. This was a humble reception for a humble Savior.

If you don't worship the Savior in an impressive cathedral, that's nothing to be ashamed of. The first Christmas was in a very lowly place with some of society's less-honored characters. That truth really struck me during my early years in the ministry. The congregation that I served had a little building, and there were not many people in attendance for the first Christmas service. That was quite a change for me, because I grew up in a large church thinking that Christmas Eve meant large crowds of people. But we don't read about a large crowd of people gathered around Jesus on that first Christmas. After Jesus had grown up, he said, "Where two or three come together in my name, there am I with them" (Matthew 18:20).

This was a small group, but did you notice that the Lord himself brought them together on that night? Mary hadn't chosen to be the mother of Jesus. God chose her to be the virgin mother of our Savior. Joseph might have chosen things to happen much differently too. His role now was to be the responsible foster father of God's Son. The shepherds hadn't planned this either. They had been minding their own business, tending their flocks, when the angel and the Lord's glory suddenly appeared. They had received a special invitation to worship the newborn Savior. The Lord had gathered this group. He did not assemble a group of the world's most powerful people. But, ironically, these humble people are now some of the most famous people in history. They will always be remembered as part of the first Christmas scene.

What will God make of you? We don't know yet. But this much we do know: Through faith in

Christ, someday you will join your Savior in heaven. There is no privilege on earth greater than that.

The First Christmas Outreach

***When they had seen him, they spread the word concerning what had been told them about this child.* (Luke 2:17)**

The shepherds knew that the good news was for "all the people" (Luke 2:10). As soon as they had seen their Redeemer, "they spread the word." They talked about what the angel had told them about Jesus. "Today in the town of David a Savior has been born to you; he is Christ the Lord."

The shepherds were the first people to do Christmas outreach. It was the angel who first declared the Christmas gospel, but the shepherds were the first to reach out with the good news of Christmas. What a privilege it was to do this work!

For a moment, think about the shepherds' training. They didn't attend any workshops or seminars. They didn't need the latest program, or method, of outreach. They didn't do advanced demographic studies. They didn't read books by outreach experts. They were simply filled with faith, and they knew the good news the angel proclaimed. They knew Jesus. So they told others about his birth. They probably said something like this: "Today in the town of David a Savior has been born to you; he is Christ the Lord."

Sometimes I fear that outreach is seen as a great and difficult burden instead of a joyful task that is inspired and directed by the Holy Spirit. If you knew that there was a certain cure for cancer, wouldn't you just love to tell that news to a dying cancer patient? I would love to have that job! "Excuse me. Sir, I've been asked to tell you that there is a complete cure for your cancer. You are going to live!" How exciting it would be to do this! It would be hard to contain my joy if I knew that my message would bring great relief to a troubled person.

Personally, I have a task that is even better, and more important too. I am called to be a pastor. Through a Christian congregation, Christ Jesus has called me to proclaim the saving gospel to people. A cure for cancer is only good for this life. Eventually, every cured cancer patient will die. But the gospel declares that Jesus has saved us from an eternity of torment in hell! The gospel brings relief that lasts forever.

This work isn't just for shepherds or pastors. Jesus wants all Christians to tell friends and relatives about God's forgiveness through his redeeming work. It should be an even greater joy to us, and an even more urgent task, than telling a dying cancer patient that a cure for his or her disease has been found. "Sir, I've got great news. You don't have to perish! Jesus saved you from sin. He lived for you and died for you. He paid for all of your sins and rose from death. You are forgiven. Whoever believes in Jesus will go to heaven. Believe in the Lord Jesus, and you too will be saved."

God uses the gospel to work faith in people's hearts. He used the gospel to work faith in the shepherd's hearts. He moved them to want to tell others the good news about Jesus. Today, when we tell others the good news of Jesus, the Holy Spirit still works through that message. "Faith comes from hearing the message" (Romans 10:17). Let's reach out to others with the saving gospel. Maybe you can be a missionary to someone you know, perhaps a child or even a grandchild. May God bless your mission work, in Jesus' name.

The Reaction to the First Christmas Outreach

And all who heard it were amazed at what the shepherds said to them. **(Luke 2:18)**

What would you think if some lowly shepherds came up to you and excitedly told you they had seen angels and the Lord himself? What would you say if they told you that the Son of God had been born in a barn? Would you think it strange if they told you that the baby in the feeding trough is your Savior and Lord?

Perhaps some of the people who heard the shepherd's message thought it strange. We are only told that people "were amazed at what the shepherds said to them." They wondered about what these shepherds said. How many people believed? We are not told. Perhaps many; perhaps few.

We don't read that a crowd gathered and worshiped Jesus. We don't read that word spread to Jerusalem, though it might have. All we know is that people wondered about the shepherds' words.

Not everyone believes when the gospel is preached. "Many are invited, but few are chosen" (Matthew 22:14). Jesus was the perfect preacher, but even when he preached, there were many who did not believe (see John 6:60-71 for one example). When Paul was in Athens, he preached to some Greek unbelievers. When he finished preaching, some "sneered" and only "a few . . . became followers" (Acts 17:32-34).

When God's Word is proclaimed, we are not responsible for the results. That is the Holy Spirit's area of responsibility, not ours. If people believe, God gets the credit. If they refuse to believe, they receive the blame. That is what Scripture teaches.

Unbelievers cannot become believers by their own thinking or choosing. God brings people to faith. In John 6:44, Jesus said, "No one can come to me unless the Father who sent me draws him, and I will raise him up at the last day." Scripture also says, "No one can say, 'Jesus is Lord,' except by the Holy Spirit" (1 Corinthians 12:3). If people believe, God has worked that belief in them through his means of grace (the gospel in Word and sacrament). Ephesians 2:8,9 explains, "For it is by grace you have been saved, through faith—and this not from yourselves, it is the gift of God—not by works, so that no one can boast." Faith and salvation are gifts from God, given purely out of his grace.

However, it is possible to reject God's gifts. If people do this, it is their fault, not God's. Jesus said, "O Jerusalem, Jerusalem, you who kill the prophets and stone those sent to you, how often I have longed to gather your children together, as a hen gathers her chicks under her wings, but you were not willing" (Matthew 23:37). The martyr Stephen said to the unbelieving Jews, "You stiff-necked people . . . you are just like your fathers: You always resist the Holy

Spirit!" (Acts 7:51). May God keep us from ever resisting the Holy Spirit!

Our Lord has given us the gospel, and faith in the gospel, so that we can look forward to heaven. He has also given us the same glorious task he gave to the angels and to the shepherds, the task of proclaiming the gospel to others. Jesus said, "Go into all the world and preach the good news to all creation. Whoever believes and is baptized will be saved, but whoever does not believe will be condemned" (Mark 16:15,16). How blessed we are to have the gospel, and faith, and this glorious task!

The Memories

***But Mary treasured up all these things and pondered them in her heart.* (Luke 2:19)**

Sometimes pictures help us to remember. When I look at pictures of my childhood or watch home movies, it brings back many memories.

Mary did not even have a snapshot of the first Christmas. There were no home movies either. But she would remember this time and what had happened here for the rest of her life. She "treasured up" everything that had happened and "pondered" the memories in her heart.

She would remember how the angel Gabriel

had appeared to her and had announced that she would be the mother of our Savior (Luke 1:26-38). She would remember visiting Elizabeth and the forerunner in Elizabeth's womb (Luke 1:39-56). She would remember marrying Joseph after each of them considered the impact of "public disgrace" (Matthew 1:18-25). She would remember the journey to Bethlehem and the fact that there was no room for them in the inn during those trying times of her life. She would remember her pregnancy and the birth of our Lord. She would remember wrapping the baby Messiah in swaddling clothes and placing him in a manger. She would remember the shepherds and their words. She would treasure up all these things and more and ponder them in her heart. Jesus was, after all, not only her son but also her Savior and Lord. There was much to think about!

Do you ponder these things each Christmas? Do you take a break from your busy preparations—the decorating, the feasting, the buying, the partying—to treasure up all these things and really ponder them?

How long would it take to read through Luke chapter 2? It would be a few minutes well spent each Christmas. Leave yourself time to really think about Luke's words and what happened. Read the account in Matthew chapter 1. We have so many distractions that it is rare for people to ponder anything anymore. There always seems to be music blaring or a television show or movie to see. These things distract us. Try to imagine what the first Christmas was really like. Picture it in your mind. Then remember what was so important about that first Christmas.

The verb in the original language indicates that Mary "kept on" pondering and remembering these thoughts. She did it over and over again. It would be good for us to do the same. When we remember and think about the gospel of Jesus Christ, the Holy Spirit can use this to strengthen our faith.

One commentator put it this way, "All the people 'wondered,' but Mary thought on all the wonderful things that happened to herself and to the shepherds. . . . Few there are who take the time to meditate upon the great facts of our salvation, to move them back and forth in their hearts, to examine them from all sides, to discover all the beauties of these priceless treasures."[4]

That is one of the ways the Holy Spirit can work in our hearts. He works through the message of the gospel, but the gospel does not only come through

---

[4]Kretzmann, Paul E. *Popular Commentary of the Bible*. (New Testament, Vol. 1). St. Louis: Concordia, 1921, pp. 273,274.

our ears. We can also read it. We can remember it as we sing hymns or even when we see symbols that depict it. And we can remember the gospel by pondering God's saving truth in our hearts. Mary was known for this (Luke 2:51). Ponder the good news! Think about it often. It is more pleasant than childhood memories, and infinitely more valuable too.

Conclusion: The Christmas Glow Remains

The shepherds returned, glorifying and praising God for all the things they had heard and seen, which were just as they had been told. **(Luke 2:20)**

"The shepherds returned." Much had happened. They had heard the angel's Christmas message. They had seen their Savior in the manger. Now the shepherds were "glorifying and praising God." These believers returned to work with new joy, the joy of salvation.

They had learned of peace with God through Jesus. They had seen their Redeemer and had become missionaries. Perhaps they would always be missionaries. They would certainly be witnesses to their friends and neighbors as they told and retold their story over the years. What a unique and amazing experience to talk about! They had seen the newborn Christ with their very own eyes. They had heard an angel talk to them. They had heard the angel choir praise God.

They now had faith through the gospel. They now returned to their station in life. They were shepherds, still shepherds. And yet they were not the same. A certain Christmas glow remained. It wasn't visible. You couldn't have seen it. But it was there. The good news of Christmas continued to burn like a flame in their hearts. In a sense, they would always take with them "the true Christmas" wherever they went. Tending sheep would never be the same again. What stories they would tell as they sat outside, watching their flocks! They would be true stories of how God had brought them to Jesus.

The true Christmas is not something in a box. It's not even a time of year, really. It is the peace and joy of knowing that God's Son was born to win forgiveness and eternal life for us. He came to prepare a place for us in heaven. Christians can take comfort in knowing that Christmas is all about God's love and that, thanks to Jesus, we don't have to be afraid of God. By faith in Jesus, "we have peace with God" (Romans 5:1).

No matter what your station in life might be, no matter where you live, take the true Christmas with you. Live the way you believe. "Rejoice in the Lord always," not just at Christmas (Philippians 4:4). No matter where you are and no matter what you do, may you always be found "glorifying and praising God." When the gospel pervades all of life, the Christmas glow will remain.

The "glorifying and praising" could be inside of us as we silently ponder the events as Mary did. The glorifying and praising could be visible as we put up manger scenes at Christmastime. The glorifying and praising could be in our hearts as we hear the Christmas gospel each year or on our lips as we sing praises in worship services. The glorifying and praising could be evident in our humble, confident, joyful attitudes as we remember our baptisms or return forgiven from the Lord's Supper. The glorifying and praising could be revealed in faithful work, even as the shepherds returned to their jobs and continued "glorifying and praising God for all the things they had heard and seen."

When you think about it, Christmas is really not about a once-a-year celebration. Our Savior is born! He came to redeem us! May the Christmas glow always remain in our hearts.